FOLENS PHOTOPACK VICTORIAN CHILDREN

Steve Harrison   **Jonathan Hewitt**

Contents

INTRODUCTION

The publisher has made every effort to contact copyright holders. If any have been overlooked, we will be pleased to make any necessary arrangements.

Folens books are protected by international copyright laws. All rights are reserved. The copyright of all materials in this book, except where otherwise stated, remains the property of the publisher and authors. No part of this publication may be reproduced, stored in a retrieval system, or transmitted, in any form or by any means, for whatever purpose, without the written permission of Folens Limited.

Folens do allow photocopying of pages marked 'copiable page', providing that this use is within the confines of the purchasing institution. Copiable pages should not be declared in any return in respect of any photocopying licence.

This resource may be used in a variety of ways. However, it is not intended that teachers or children should write directly into the book itself.

British Library Cataloguing in Publication Data. A catalogue record for this book is available from the British Library.

Steve Harrison and Jonathan Hewitt hereby assert their moral rights to be identified as the authors of this work in accordance with the Copyright, Designs and Patents Act 1988.
© 1997 Folens Limited, on behalf of the authors.

Editor: Claire Ancell
Layout Artist: Pat Hollingsworth
Cover image: Barnardo's Photographic Archive
Cover design: In Touch Creative Services Ltd

The authors and publisher would like to thank the following for permission to reproduce the following photographs:
Photo 1 © Mrs M Wemyss
Photo 2 © Manchester Central Library, Local Studies Unit
Photo 3 © Hulton Getty
Photo 4 © The Mansell Collection
Photo 5 © The Salvation Army International Heritage Centre
Photo 6 © Hulton Getty
Photo 7 © Manchester Central Library, Local Studies Unit
Photo 8 © Barnardo's Photographic Archive
Photo 9 © The Salvation Army International Heritage Centre
Photo 10 © Hulton Getty
A2 Poster: Mining © Mary Evans Picture Library
Shoeshine boy © Greenwich Local History Library
Canal work © Manchester Central Library, Local Studies Unit
Hop picking © Hampshire County Museum Service
Chimney sweep © Mary Evans Picture Library
Matchseller © Barnardo's Photographic Archive
Page 15 Both pictures © The Illustrated London News Picture Library
Page 16 © Mary Evans Picture Library

First published 1997 by Folens Limited, Dunstable and Dublin.
Folens Limited, Albert House, Apex Business Centre, Boscombe Road, Dunstable, LU5 4RL, England.

ISBN 185276571-2

Printed in the United Kingdom.

The Victorian age was a time of immense change as the population shifted from the countryside to the towns and cities, creating a world of mass production and making Britain the world's leading industrial power.

In the midst of all this change the population grew prodigiously, doubling between 1850 and 1901, the end of Queen Victoria's reign. A society was created in which children played a major role. The photographs and illustrations in this pack aim to provide opportunities to explore this role and, in studying the lives of children and their families, the chance to explore a range of themes essential to developing an understanding of Victorian Britain.

The study of family life illustrates the great chasm that existed between the rich and the poor in Victorian society, and highlights the very different roles of boys and girls. It is important to remember, however, that society not only consisted of the very rich and the destitute, but that there were many families who were striving to maintain and enhance their quality of life. Homelessness and poverty were common, and this led both to the work of a great many charitable organisations to assist the needy and to the great emigrations to North America and Australasia in search of a new start.

Discussion of the harsh realities of child labour can be upsetting. Explore the part that many children played in supplementing the family's income by working in the sweated trades, and their exploitation in some of the major industries. At the same time, however, the late nineteenth century saw the birth of compulsory education and early steps on the road to a literate society.

As we study an era of change it is important that we remind the children that many of these images represent the lives of real people with hopes and fears, and that we work to develop an understanding of what it was like to be a Victorian child.

Each page in this book contains background information, starting points for introducing the photographs, key questions for teachers to ask and ideas for activities.

While the photographs in the pack are all black and white, the illustration 'Doll makers and doll breakers' is in colour. It might be useful to point out that at this time photography was in its early stages, while colour illustrations were long-established.

The photographs have not been labelled, in order to stimulate lines of enquiry and allow children to use visual clues to make deductions.

WORK

Poster
© Mary Evans Picture Library,
© Greenwich Local History Library,
© Manchester Central Library, Local Studies Unit,
© Hampshire County Museum Service,
© Mary Evans Picture Library,
© Barnardo's Photographic Archive

Victorian children at work

The poster shows children working in different environments.

Picture 1 shows two children being lowered down a mine shaft so that they can pull the wagons loaded with coal. These two children were interviewed by members of a Royal Commission, who were shocked by the brutality with which the children were treated.

Picture 2 shows a shoeshine boy. Shining shoes on the streets was linked to the awful state of the roads. It is still common in the wider world today.

Picture 3 shows a gang of boys working on the Manchester Ship Canal as labourers. Although the work was hard they were grateful for a regular, if small, wage while they were employed.

Picture 4 illustrates that children were put to work in the countryside as well as in the towns, in this case to pick hops. When picking in the fields, gangs of women and children often worked under the supervision of a gangmaster, who preferred them because he could pay them less than male labourers.

Picture 5 shows a chimney sweep. The reformers' main concern was for boys who were forced to climb chimneys – many only 30cm square. Legislation against boy sweeps was passed in the nineteenth century but two thousand remained as late as 1867.

Picture 6 shows a young girl selling matches on the street. Although the wages were pitiful many children worked in this way to supplement the family income. This picture is posed but it reflects real life.

Starting points

◆ Ask the pupils to describe the type of work the children are doing in each of the pictures.
◆ They should consider the dangers involved in each job.

Job	Description	Dangers
Selling matches	Girl standing on pavement selling matches to passers-by. Barefoot in all weather conditions – illness.	Danger from talking to strangers.

Key questions

1. Do you think the children are enjoying their work? Explain your answer.
2. Why do the employers want to employ women and children instead of men?
3. Are there any differences between the work of boys and girls?
4. Do you think the work is dangerous? Explain why.
5. Do you think all these pictures are from the Victorian period? Why do you think so?
6. Do you think any of the pictures could be misleading? If so, which?
7. Which of these jobs is still carried out today? By whom? (Think of the wider world as well as the UK.)

Activities

● Discuss with the children ways in which you could find out whether the pictures are giving an authentic view of children at work. Brainstorm some evidence that might be helpful, such as other pictures of children at work, written records and reference books.
● Read to the children this extract from an interview with the boy in picture 3 in 1842.

"She goes down with us into the mine. I have seen her thrashed many times; they rap her in the face and knock her down. She does not like her work. I have seen her cry many times. She says she will be killed before she leaves the coal pit."

● Ask the children to choose one of the pictures and to find out more about it so that they can present some evidence to a Royal Commission on Child Labour. They could include conditions, hours of work, treatment, danger, pay, age of workers and why they do it.

BATHTIME

During the late nineteenth century there was no running water in most of the homes occupied by the poorer people. Water was, in fact, a valuable commodity and was often brought in buckets from standpipes in the kitchen or the yard. Few homes had bathrooms and a bath was a weekly event where the children squeezed into a tin tub in front of the fire using water heated on the stove or range. Many houses did not have main sewers and the waste water was often poured into an open sewer outside. The photograph shows children being bathed in a mining household around 1890. It is interesting to note that it is the eldest daughter and not the mother who is responsible for bathing the children. In many poor homes the eldest girl was given a great deal of responsibility for the younger children and the running of the house while the mother was out at work. Bathtimes such as this persisted widely until the 1950s. It is not purely a Victorian phenomenon.

Many elder siblings still take responsibility for the younger family members, particularly in the economically developing world.

Starting points

◆ Ask the children to identify the main features of the photograph and discuss their uses.

Feature	Use
Kitchen range	Cooking, heating water
Wooden box	Holding soap
Bucket	
Bath	

◆ Discuss the photograph and consider how we know that it is from a long time ago. Clues could include: range, metal bucket, tin bath, clothes.

Key questions

1. What is happening in the photograph?
2. How is the water heated?
3. Why is the bath in the kitchen?
4. Who is bathing the youngest child? Why?
5. Where do you think the mother is? Why?
6. Do you think the family is rich or poor? Give a reason for your answer.

Activities

● Explain to the children that many houses did not have a water supply. Water companies provided water for an area for a limited time each day. This water had to be paid for and carried to the home. In many cases this was not clean water but water drawn from dirty rivers.
● In order to help the children to understand the difficulties of maintaining a high level of sanitation with limited running water, ask them to find out how much water they use each day for drinking, cooking, washing, flushing toilets and so on. They can estimate how many buckets of water they would need.

Activity	Buckets needed
Bath	10
Toilet flush (8 times)	8
Cleaning teeth	$\frac{1}{4}$

● Ask the children to imagine that they have been told to organise the weekly bathtime for their younger brothers or sisters and write an account of what they needed to do.

RICH CHILDREN AT PLAY

The children of upper and middle-class families lived a comfortable existence in Victorian Britain. They were well fed and clothed and had fine toys to keep them amused. They often spent a great deal of time in a nursery or schoolroom at the top of the house under the watchful eye of a resident 'nurse' or 'nanny'.

These children were not expected to go out to work as children, but were prepared for their role in society. Boys and girls were, however, treated very differently. Boys were generally provided with the opportunity of a good education which began at home with a governess and continued at one of the public schools. Such an education was often regarded as wasted on girls who instead were taught the social graces in preparation for marriage. The photograph shows children playing at Alkrington Hall, an imposing family residence set in substantial grounds.

Starting points

◆ Ask the children to look at the photograph and discuss whether the children are rich or poor, giving reasons for their hypotheses.
◆ Consider how such a large house could be maintained, the need for servants and how the children benefited.

Workers in a rich home		
Job	Description	How rich children benefited
Maid	General cleaning duties	Kept the children's rooms clean and tidy
Governess	Educated children in the home	Individual teaching

◆ The children could research the jobs done, for example: cook, butler, gardener, coachman.

Activities

● The children's rooms often had samplers showing wise sayings hanging on the wall. Give the children some of these sayings and explore their meanings, for example, 'Children should be seen and not heard'.
● The children could research some of the activities in a day in the life of a child in a place like Alkrington Hall and write an imaginary diary of their experiences. They could include some anachronisms and ask a partner to find them, for example, 'We played on the rocking horse and then listened to the radio'.
● Use a cross-section of a large Victorian residence or a Victorian dolls' house such as that in *Photopack Victorian Toys* (Folens).
  – Which rooms are for the children?
  – Where are these rooms?
  – Is there a bathroom?

Key questions

1. What are the children in the photograph doing?
2. Who do you think is in charge of the game? Why?
3. Who do you think cooks the children's meals, cleans their rooms and bathes them?
4. Why is the children's mother not in the photograph?
5. Why do the children have time to play? Why are they not at work?
6. What are the children wearing? How is this different to what poor children wore?
7. When the chimneys needed cleaning would any of these children be sent up to do the job? Explain your answer.

ROYAL BABIES

Photo 3
© Hulton Getty

This picture shows the great-grandchildren of Queen Victoria, Edward and George. Edward went on to become Edward VIII, who abdicated in 1936 without ever being crowned, and George became George VI in 1936 upon his brother's abdication. He was the father of Queen Elizabeth II. The two boys are wearing dresses. All babies (boys and girls) were dressed alike during the late nineteenth century.

The photograph also illustrates the Victorian concern to keep babies away from fresh air by the way that they are heavily clothed. The prams are clearly carefully crafted with coachwork bodies and springs to provide a smoother ride for the young princes. It is interesting, however, to note the solid tyres and that even royals cried and needed dummies to keep them quiet!

Starting point

- ◆ Ask the children to look closely at the photograph and try to guess who the babies might be. Encourage them to look for clues as to whether they are important people or not and to consider how old the photograph is.
  - When was photography invented?
  - What is the style of the clothes?
  - What is the style and technology of the prams?

Activity

- ● Provide the children with a family tree showing the House of Windsor. Explain how a family tree is set out. Ask the pupils to try to work out who the two babies are. You could give a series of clues and ask the children to make a guess after each clue, such as 'They are brothers.' Photography was not widely used until after 1860. They were both children of George and Mary. They were both kings. The elder lived for 78 years.

Key questions

1. Are these children from a rich or poor family?
2. Are the children boys or girls?
3. Do you think they are related?
4. Do you think this is a posed photograph? Why?
5. Do you think the children look happy?
6. Why are they so heavily dressed?

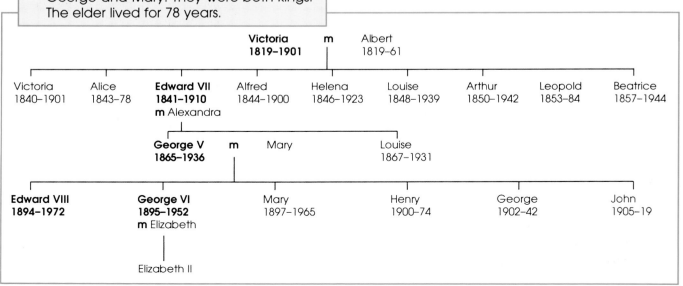

		Victoria 1819–1901	**m**	Albert 1819–61				
Victoria 1840–1901	Alice 1843–78	**Edward VII 1841–1910** **m** Alexandra	Alfred 1844–1900	Helena 1846–1923	Louise 1848–1939	Arthur 1850–1942	Leopold 1853–84	Beatrice 1857–1944

	George V 1865–1936	**m**	Mary	Louise 1867–1931	
Edward VIII 1894–1972	**George VI 1895–1952** **m** Elizabeth		Mary 1897–1965	Henry 1900–74	George 1902–42	John 1905–19

Elizabeth II

DOLL MAKERS AND DOLL BREAKERS

Photo 4
© The
Mansell
Collection

Children were employed in a wide range of occupations during the reign of Queen Victoria, and many of them were involved in what were called the 'sweated trades'. These children generally worked in small workshops called 'sweatshops', where they produced a variety of goods for a contractor. Children were often employed because they were cheap. The wages were very poor and were directly related to the amount of work completed. Acts of Parliament in the middle and late nineteenth century regulated the hours that children could work, but children in sweated trades often worked very long hours for a wage of around three shillings (15p) per week. The pictures show the great difference between poor and rich children, with the poor children providing the playthings for the rich.

Photo 4 is a contemporary illustration. Its vivid colours could be used as a contrast to the photographs of the period, which are black and white as photography was in its infancy during the Victorian age.

Starting points

◆ Ask the children to compare the two pictures and discuss the different experiences of rich and poor children.

Picture 1	Picture 2
Children working	Children playing
Children look serious	Children look happy
Poor clothes	Very good clothes
Children carefully make toys	Children do not look after their toys

◆ Discuss how the pictures make the pupils feel.

Key questions

Picture 1
1. What are the children making?
2. Why do you think that the contractor employs children?
3. Do you think the children are well paid? Give reasons.

Picture 2
4. What are the children's toys?
5. Why are these children not working?
6. Are they looking after their toys? Why not?
7. What do you think the picture is trying to tell us? Is it successful?

Activities

● Tell the children that this picture appeared in a magazine called *Punch*. Ask them to write an article based upon the picture to show the differences between rich and poor children.
Discuss with the children whether this evidence gives a fair picture of all rich children. Do they think that all the rich children did not care about their toys or other people? They could find some pictures of rich children behaving very formally and properly and contrast the two different views.
● *Punch* magazine was launched in 1841. Always noted for its humour, it has featured many writers with a strong moral conscience. In the early days Mayhew (*London Labour and the London Poor*) wrote for *Punch*. His contributions had been shunned by other publications.
● Ask the children to research stories such as *The Little Match Girl* or folk songs such as 'Fourpence a Day' to explore the way that children were exploited in employment. Discuss why the children worked for such little reward.

WORK IN THE HOME

Photo 5
© The Salvation Army
International Heritage
Centre

In the 1880s and 1890s the average family had six children, but it was common to have ten, twelve or more. In addition, many babies were born but did not survive – one in five died at birth and one in four died before their first birthday. Many working-class women had to carry on taking care of their large families directly after giving birth, putting a great strain on their health. Men could not increase their earnings, so another mouth to feed meant a little less for everyone. Many women worked at home to supplement the family's income, doing repetitive tasks like making brushes or placing safety pins in cards. Rates of pay were very low and depended upon the amount of work done. For example, $2\frac{1}{2}$d (1p) was paid for a gross (144) of cards of safety pins. Older children often helped with the work while the eldest girl looked after the younger children. The photograph shows a mother and children making brushes in the 1890s. Families feared being unable to pay the rent, as homeless families could be sent to the workhouse where they would be given shelter but could be split up.

Starting points

◆ Ask the pupils to discuss whether the family in the photograph is rich or poor, giving reasons for their answers.

Evidence	Deduction
Working at home to earn money	Low earnings for many hours' work. Mum could probably have earned more in a factory but would then need to pay someone to look after the children.
Wallpaper and pictures	Desperately poor people would not have been able to afford a home with these. The father probably worked.
Furniture	Very little and old. Probably most of the money earned went on food for the family.
Clothes and shoes	Look old and worn.

◆ Discuss with the pupils that many families were neither rich nor very poor but were able to afford some luxuries and took pride in their homes. It is worth contrasting this with the common view that people in Victorian Britain were either very rich or living in total poverty.

Key questions

1. How many children are in the family?
2. How old do you think they are?
3. What is the family making?
4. Which child is working with the mother?
5. What are the others doing?
6. Why do you think the children are not at school?
7. Why is the mother working at home?
8. How do you think childhood could have been more enjoyable?

Activities

● Ask the children to find out the average number of children in their families and compare this with the average in Victorian Britain (5.8 children). The results could be represented graphically.
● Discuss with them the advantages/disadvantages of having a greater/fewer number of children in a family.
● Ask the children to find out about life in the workhouse and consider what it would be like to be split up as a family. The children could explore these issues through role play. They may be able to understand why people were prepared to accept such appalling wages and long hours in order to stay together as a family. Remember too that the philosophy of the workhouse was that it should never provide accommodation which might attract the feckless to an easy life!

SCHOOL

Photo 6
© Hulton Getty

In the early nineteenth century, working-class children were educated in Sunday schools, and increasingly in schools operating under the 'monitorial' system. This system depended on private, charitable finance to fund the building and teacher costs. Costs were low because most of the tuition was provided by monitors, as Joseph Lancaster (a Quaker founder of one of the monitorial systems) wrote in 1803:

The boys are instructed upon a plan entirely new: by means of which ONE MASTER alone can educate 1000 boys in Reading, Writing and Arithmetic as easily and with as little trouble as twenty or thirty have ever been taught by the usual methods.

Government support for monitorial schools began in 1833. However, no support was available for the poorest areas where no charitable schools had been established. Various Christian denominations and Jewish societies established schools during the Victorian period, attracting subsequent government grants. By the 1860s the amount of money being spent was regarded as too much. The 'Payment by Results' system was introduced in part to reduce government expenditure.

Industrial competition from Germany and the USA led to demands for a better educated workforce not dependent on the distribution of charitably-based schools. The 1870 Education Act forced local ratepayers to elect school boards which could raise a local rate and build schools. Initially children paid a small fee, but this was later dropped. Once established, these schools became compulsory for five to eleven-year-olds.

The photograph shows children exercising in a classroom in 1883.

Starting point

◆ Compare the photograph of the school with schools today, for example:

Victorian times	Today
Pupils all in one room.	Pupils in separate classes.
Pupils in rows of bench seats.	Pupils with desks or tables.
Little displayed on the walls.	Bright, colourful displays.
Children working on slates.	Children use paper, pencils and computers.
Boys and girls are separate.	Boys and girls are together.

Key questions

1. How many classrooms can you see? Why is it so crowded?
2. Who do you think is in charge?
3. How many teachers can you see?
4. Why do you think they use tiered benches?
5. Why are the boys and girls kept separate?
6. Why is there so little of the children's work displayed?
7. Why do you think that the teacher had to be very strict?
8. Do you think this is a posed photograph? Explain your answer.

Activities

● Ask the children to look at page 16. Discuss the following:
   – What subject is this teaching?
   – What does it tell us about the roles of boys and girls in Victorian times?
● Ask the children to answer the questions in silence. You could use small chalk boards and slate pencils to record the answers.
● Brainstorm with the children a range of evidence about schools in Victorian times and try to find some of this evidence for a local school. (Log book, school photographs, personal memories, old lessons, textbooks and so on.) What does it tell them?

ON THE BEAT

Photo 7
© Manchester
Central Library,
Local Studies Unit

The nineteenth century saw rapid developments in the police forces of most towns and cities. Although they were involved in fighting crime, policemen also played an important role in the local communities, becoming familiar figures in the areas they patrolled on foot. Amongst their community duties, policemen looked after children at the beginning and end of the school day. Most children in the towns lived close to their schools and walked to school each day. Many of the children were unaccompanied as their parents were already at work by that time. Although there was relatively little traffic, the local policeman would act as a crossing patrol.

The photograph shows a policeman in the City of London force, in Lower Ormond Street. It was taken in approximately 1900. He is clearly well-known and liked by the children.

Starting point

◆ Ask the children to look at the photograph and compare the scene with school crossing arrangements today. Children will not necessarily be aware that the duties of crossing wardens and traffic wardens were once carried out by police officers.

Feature	Victorian times	Today
Traffic		
Road surface		
Crossing patrol		
Adults		
Road markings		
Clothing of policeman		
Clothing of children		
Behaviour of children		

Key questions

1. What is the policeman doing?
2. Why is the policeman needed?
3. Do you think the children like the policeman? How can you tell?
4. Why are there no parents collecting the children?
5. Do you think the streets were safer for children then? How could you find out?
6. What do you think is the age range of the children who attend the school?
7. Why do you think all the pupils are walking?

Activities

● Ask the pupils to compare the role of the crossing patrol today with that of 100 years ago. The pupils could take photographs of a crossing warden and compare them with the policeman, discussing such details as clothes and equipment and giving reasons for their use. Does the policeman have the advantage of a zebra or pelican crossing and/or yellow flashing warning lights? Why were these items not common in 1900? (Think about technology and traffic volume.)
● Ask the children to map where everyone in the class lives. Do they all live very near to the school? Is this similar to or different from the Victorian age?

● Create a graph to show how pupils come to school, for example: walk accompanied, walk unaccompanied, car, bicycle, bus. Ask them to compare their findings with the scene in the photograph and explain the differences.

DR BARNARDO'S CHILDREN

Photo 8
© Barnardo's
Photographic
Archive

Homelessness was a great problem amongst young people in the towns and cities because many families lived in poverty and could not earn enough to support themselves. As a result, many children left home and slept on the streets. The problem was exacerbated by the large number of young people who experienced poverty in the countryside and went to the towns in search of work and lodgings, but failed to find either when they arrived.

Dr Thomas Barnardo (1845–1905) was born in Dublin and did evangelising work in the slums there as a teenager. He moved to London as a missionary medical student. He qualified as a doctor and practised in the East End of London. He was appalled by the number of destitute and homeless children. He created a home for homeless boys in 1867 in Stepney, and a home for girls in Barkingside in 1876. In 1882 he arranged for destitute children to go to Canada to start new lives in the Colonies. By the time he died, in 1905, there were 112 homes which had helped over 60 000 children. He once refused a boy entry to his home because it was full and, upon finding that the boy had died, he decided that no boy should ever be refused again.

This photograph was used to publicise Dr Barnardo's work and clearly has a painted backcloth – it is not an actual event but a form of propaganda designed to evoke outrage at the dreadful conditions and raise financial support for alleviating them.

Starting points

- ◆ Ask the children to look at the photograph and describe how they feel (happy, sad, angry, sympathetic).
- ◆ The children could consider what the photograph is trying to achieve. Is it successful in persuading them that they should try to help homeless children?

Key questions

1. Was sleeping on the streets common in Victorian Britain?
2. How can you find out?
3. Why did people do this?
4. How has the boy tried to make himself comfortable?
5. What dangers would such children have been in?
6. What do you think happened to people sleeping rough in a very severe winter?
7. How do you think boys like this obtained money?
8. Are there any homeless people today?
9. Are there more in some countries than others? Why?

Activities

- ● Discuss whether this photograph is genuine or posed. What clues tell us that this is not a real street but a scene produced in a studio? Is this an acceptable way of raising money? What are the dangers?
- ● Encourage the children to recreate a scene from the past. This can be photographed in black and white and tried out with another class or school as a genuine piece of historical evidence. The key is to keep it simple, using old walls or buildings as a backdrop.
- ● Research the story of Dr Barnardo and find out why Barnardo's motto is 'No child ever turned away'.
- ● Ask the pupils to create their own publicity material to try to persuade people to give money to support the homes of Dr Barnardo.

FEED LONDON'S HOMELESS CHILDREN

THE SALVATION ARMY

Photo 9
© The Salvation Army
International Heritage
Centre

While poverty was widespread in the villages, towns and cities of Victorian Britain, the young and old were affected the most. Families were generally large, and young children often proved to be a drain upon resources at a time when they were too young to work themselves and made it difficult for their mother to earn a reasonable wage. Clothes were often ill-fitting because they were passed from child to child, and many children did not have a decent pair of shoes. Faced with large-scale childhood poverty, groups like the Waifs and Strays Society of the Church of England and the Salvation Army offered cheap or free food at hostels. The photograph shows children queuing for 'farthing breakfasts' at a Salvation Army hostel in London. Such ventures were not without their critics, who claimed that charity would create an idle class who never needed to work for a living.

The Salvation Army is an international Christian organisation. It was founded in 1865 in London by William Booth. The 'military' uniform is worn on special occasions. The emphasis for members is on personal morality rather than on particular doctrines. The Salvation Army rejects the sacraments. It is world famous for its social and missionary work.

Starting points

◆ Compare the children in this picture with the children outside Alkrington Hall (photo 2).

	Alkrington Hall	Outside the Salvation Army hostel
Ages		
Clothes		
Hair		
Environment		

◆ Discuss with the children the reasons why the children in the photograph are queuing. Ask them to look for clues.

Key questions

1. Are the children rich or poor? Explain your answer.
2. Why do you think the children were poor?
3. Why do you think the children's clothes are so ill-fitting?
4. Do you think these children attended this hostel regularly? How do you know?
5. How do you think the children feel as they queue for food?
6. Why do you think there are no adults in the queue?

Activities

● Tell the class that the children in the picture are queuing for 'farthing breakfasts'. Ask them to find out what these were and why they were so popular.
● Give the children this chart and ask them to think of reasons why change may have occurred.

1880s	1980s	Possible reasons for change
500 out every 100 000 mothers died giving birth	15 out of every 100 000 mothers died giving birth	
15 in every 60 children died in the first year	1 in every 60 children died in the first year	
School leaving age – 13 years	School leaving age – 16 years	

BY THE SEASIDE

Photo 10
© Hulton
Getty

In the early nineteenth century seaside holidays were largely the preserve of the rich. The opening of the railways, in the 1840s, gave families the opportunity to visit the seaside on day trips on bank holidays. It was generally believed that the sea air was healthy and would benefit the whole family, especially those living in sooty, grimy factory towns.

Children enjoyed a range of activities including playing on the beach, going on donkey rides, rowing boats and watching the Punch and Judy show. Most children were well covered, even on the beach, as it was thought immodest to be scantily clad. Even when people bathed they often changed in a bathing machine which was then pulled into the sea so that the occupants could slip into the water unseen. As most resorts were only busy for a short period of time, local people were often involved in fishing and the beaches were working beaches. Tourism as an industry was in its infancy. People earned extra money from day trippers, but were not dependent upon them. Many trippers brought their own food for the day. Even when weekend breaks became popular in later Victorian times, enough food for the whole break would be carried by the family on the train. Tea shops did better business than restaurants!

The photograph shows families visiting Freshwater Bay, on the Isle of Wight.

Starting point

◆ Ask the children to comment upon some of the features in the picture and consider why they are present.

Features	Why they are there
Dinghies	
Canoes	
Bathing machines	
Slipway	
Lobster pots	

Key questions

1. What are the children doing?
2. How are the children dressed?
3. Why do you think they are so well-dressed?
4. What evidence is there that people use this beach for work?
5. Do you think that this resort is a very busy one? Explain your answer.
6. What is on this beach which you would not find on a beach today?
7. What is on this beach which you might find on a beach today?
8. What is not on this beach which you would find on a beach today?

Activities

● Explain that families from towns and cities went to the local seaside resorts. By using an atlas the children can identify the nearest resorts to their own town, and which towns and cities were served by the following resorts:

Southend
Weston-super-Mare
Aberystwyth
Scarborough

Blackpool
Ayr
Brighton
Great Yarmouth

● Discuss the reasons why the railways were so important in enabling large numbers of families to spend days at the seaside.
● Ask the children to research all the activities that people did at the seaside and create a poster advertising a Victorian resort.

EMIGRATION

During the reign of Queen Victoria millions of people emigrated from Europe to America, Canada, Australia and New Zealand. The great majority of emigrants crossed the Atlantic to America, with many families sailing from Liverpool. Until the middle of the nineteenth century most of the crossings were made by sailing ships, although later on steam ships completed the journey in about one fifth of the time. People emigrated for a variety of reasons but most left to escape poverty, persecution or to further their ambitions. Having made the decision to emigrate, most families were faced with an unpredictable and often unpleasant crossing as they travelled in crowded accommodation for up to 35 days. On arrival, few people had jobs to go to and most families struggled for the first few years in their new home.

The copiable pictures on page 15 show conditions on the Liverpool dockside in 1850, and accommodation arrangements on an emigrant ship.

Starting points

◆ Discuss the idea of emigration with the pupils. Ask them to describe how different members of the family might feel as they prepare to leave their home, for example:
  – a father who has lost his job or been thrown off the land
  – a mother who has brought up two young children who might never see their grandparents again
  – children who do not want to leave their friends
  – a family facing a famine (for example, the Irish potato famine).
◆ Ask the children to think of some of the reasons why people might want to emigrate.

Key questions

1. Why do you think a large number of people emigrated from Liverpool?
2. What was the attraction of North America?
3. Are most of the emigrants on the dockside men or women? Can you give a reason for this?
4. What sorts of things are they taking with them?
5. Why do you think they are taking so much luggage?
6. Do you think these emigrants are wealthy? Explain your answer.
7. Do you think the arrangements for boarding the ship are well organised? Give reasons for your answer.

Activities

● Ask the children to choose some characters in the pictures and explain why they think they are going to America.
● Look at the picture which shows conditions inside the ship for most of the people who went to America around 1850. Ask the children to brainstorm words to describe the conditions and then to consider what might make the journey so unpleasant, for example:
  crowded – The ship would be stuffy and the stench of people being seasick would be dreadful.
  dirty – The conditions were filthy and there were no toilet facilities down in the steerage of the ship. Anyone who became ill could easily pass on their illness to the other passengers.
  dangerous – The only light would come from lanterns which could cause a serious fire in a wooden ship.
● Ask the pupils to imagine that they are travelling to America in the steerage of a sailing ship and to describe their journey using the picture to help them.

EMIGRANTS LEAVING FOR AMERICA

Courtesy of The Illustrated London News Picture Library

PHOTOPACK – *Victorian Children*

PAGE FROM A VICTORIAN TEXTBOOK

PHOTOPACK – *Victorian Children*